Josef Moser

Ubuntu 18.04

Quick Guide
for Beginners

Illustration: Josef Moser
Coverdesign: Jutta Moser und Josef Moser

Publisher:
[JMP] Josef Moser Publishing, Ulmenstr. 55, 90537 Feucht
Printed by: Amazon
KDPISBN: 978-1-0916-7439-4

Contents

1. Foreword

This book is **Volume 1** of

The Linux Beginner Series.

Many computer users are mainly familiar with Microsoft Windows or Apple MacOS.
Linux, on the other hand, is generally regarded as difficult to access and only suitable for hobbyists and tinkerers.
I would like to show in my quick guides that you do not have to be afraid to deal with this operating system.
Linux distributions have reached a very high level.
This applies not only to the operating system itself, but also to the available applications. Libre Office, for example, is a very good alternative for Microsoft Office.
There also are many very good applications for photo and film editing.
It is possible to edit photos and organize them in many different ways.
You can still use Firefox and Thunderbird to browse the web and check your emails.

Currently there are over 100 Linux distributions available to choose from.
This may be confusing to potential newcomers.

This series of books should help you get to know at least the most important distributions.

This book is intended to give you a quick and easy access to **Ubuntu 18.04**.

After some basic information this book will guide you through the operating system step by step.

I concentrate on the essential elements that are important for a home user.

After reading this book, you will be able to

- ➤ get an installation medium (ISO file) for Ubuntu 18.04
- ➤ install Ubuntu 18.04
- ➤ understand the basic settings of Ubuntu 18.04
- ➤ configure Ubuntu 18.04 to suit your needs

I would be very pleased, if I manage to get you excited about Linux in this way.

You may be surprised at the benefits a Linux system can bring.

With this in mind I hope you enjoy this book and the Linux operating system **Ubuntu 18.04**.

Josef Moser

2. What is Linux?

Linux is a family of free and open-source software operating systems based on the Linux Kernel, an operating system kernel first released on September 17, 1991 by Linus Torvalds. Linux is typically packaged in a Linux distribution (or distro for short).
Distributions include the Linux kernel and supporting system software and libraries, many of which are provided by the GNU Project.
(Source: Wikipedia.org)

The Linux kernel saw the light of day in 1991 in version 0.0.1.
Linus Torvalds, who is still in charge of kernel development today, had no idea what he would initiate with the release of his small hobby project.

Today, the term Linux is usually used as a synonym for the entire system. Strictly speaking, however, only the kernel is called Linux.
Only when combined with applications and programs that follow the GNU guidelines it becomes the system we know and love today.

The first Linux distributions were released in 1994. They had made it their business to develop usable systems as an alternative to Windows and MacOS:
Debian
Suse
Slackware
RedHat

A major step forward was the release of **Open Office** (Version 1) in 2002.
It was a full-featured open source office suite, which was available free of charge.
Of course, the functionality was still limited compared to Microsoft Office, but Open Office became better and better over time.

Libre Office has been developed at a later time as an independent fork of Open Office. This extensive and meanwhile very mature office suite is pre-installed in Ubuntu 18.04.

Meanwhile there are countless variants of Linux distributions.
However, most of them are based on Debian, Open-Suse, Ubuntu, Arch Linux, Gentoo or Red Hat.

3. What is Ubuntu?

The Linux operating system **Ubuntu** exists since 2004.
The Ubuntu project was founded by Marc Shuttleworth, a South African multimillionaire, who is also the main sponsor through his company **Canonical**.

In Zulu language, **Ubuntu** means "humanity towards others".
The focus of the project is to develop an operating system that should be available to as many people as possible all over the world.

Special attention was paid to intuitive usability and tools for universal accessibility.
Ubuntu is open source software that is available free of charge.

Since the release of the first version, the degree of recognition and popularity could be increased steadily.

Ubuntu is based on **Debian**. This means that the package management created by Debian and also the software selection has been adopted more or less.
However, over time both distributions moved away from each other.
For example, Ubuntu has often been accused of being too commercial, while Debian continued to follow the philosophy of open source, denying some of the innovations that Ubuntu introduced.

Each year in April and October a new version of Ubuntu is released, which receives **support for nine months**.

It is named after the year and month of release.

Ubuntu 18.10 was released in October (10) of 2018 (18).

Support *means that Ubuntu's operating system receives updates in the form of security updates and bug fixes.*

However, every two years (even years!) a special version is released which will receive **support** from Ubuntu for a period of **5 years**.

This is called an **LTS version**.

LTS stands for **Long-Term-Support**.

The current version is **Ubuntu 18.04**.

Support for this version will end after 5 years in **April 2023**.

The next LTS version **Ubuntu 20.04** will be released in April 2020.

Support for this version will end after 5 years in **April 2025**.

All other versions are supported for 9 months.

Ubuntu 16.04 LTS	supported until	04/2021
Ubuntu 18.04 LTS	supported until	04/2023
Ubuntu 18.10	supported until	07/2019
Ubuntu 19.04	supported until	01/2020
Ubuntu 19.10	supported until	07/2020
Ubuntu 20.04 LTS	supported unitl	04/2025

The advantage of short-term supported systems is that the software they contain is usually more up-to-date than that of the last regular LTS-version.

The LTS-version essentially remains the same for five years.
Updates only include bug fixes and security patches.
This may be too conservative for some users in the long run.
However, the older a software is, the more it is tested and therefore more stable.

Newer versions of applications, such as those included in the short-term supported versions, may be more unstable because the testing period was shorter.

In this quick guide, I describe **Ubuntu 18.04 LTS**.
Much of it is also applicable to Ubuntu 18.10 and Ubuntu 19.04.

For beginners it is recommended to try out the LTS version first.
A Shortterm- version makes sense if the LTS version does not support your hardware optimally.

In addition to the official names that refer to the release date, Ubuntu versions always have an additional fantasy name.
That is **18.04 Bionic Beaver** and **18.10 Cosmic Cuttlefish**.

4. How do you get Ubuntu?

It is always the safest way to get the required installation medium (ISO file) directly from Ubuntu.

You find it on the **Ubuntu Hmepage** in **Downloads**.

https://www.ubuntu.com/download/desktop

Select the direct link to the **64-bit** Ubuntu file.

System requirements (minimal):

2 GHz Dual Core processor or better
2 GB RAM or better
25 GB free hard disk space or more
DVD drive or USB port
Internet connection

There are also other versions (flavours) of Ubuntu available for download.
These are independent Ubuntu distributions with alternative desktops.

For example, there are

> *Kubuntu*   with KDE desktop,
> *Xubuntu*   with XFCE desktop
> *Ubuntu Mate*   with Mate Desktop.

The basic system is almost identical in all of these distributions, but the desktop envrionment looks very different in each flavour.

In contrast to the main version, the LTS versions of the "Flavours" are only supported for 3 years.

The Short-term-versions stick to the 9-month cycle.

You can check out a flavour if you do not like the design of the main version for some reason.

You can find a list of available Ubuntu flavours at the end of the book.

5. Create a bootable stick

Once you have downloaded the **ISO file**, you need to create a **bootable stick**.

This means that you have to prepare an USB-stick so that you can start Ubuntu with it.

For this task you need an appropriate program.
There are several applications that you can use for this task.

Etcher is a good choice in my opinion.
Etcher is free for Linux, Windows and MacOS.

https://www.balena.io/etcher/

Download Etcher and then create the stick.

Etcher is self-explanatory.

Select image (the ISO file for Ubuntu 18.04.)
Select drive (you will see a selection of sticks that you have plugged into a free USB port).
Choose the one you want to use for Ubuntu.
Flash (Start!)

Double check if the right stick is selected.
Any content on the stick will be completely erased!

6. Starting from Stick

You plug the stick into a free USB port and after restarting your computer the Ubuntu Live System should start.

The stick should be at the very top of the boot order in the BIOS. If the hard disk is in first place, the operating system on it will always start first and the stick will be ignored.

If that is the case, then you have to change the **boot order** in the **BIOS**.

You start the BIOS of the computer via one of the F-keys (for example [F2]). While the computer is booting, you must press this key several times. This will prevent the computer to boot. You will get into the BIOS instead.

Please look into the manual, which key is the right one for your motherboard. This varies depending on the manufacturer.

In the BIOS there is a menu called **boot** (or similar). Here you can change the boot order.

7. Installation

After successfully launching the ISO file from your stick, you select the language.

On the left side you first set the desired language.
Since English is usually the default, activate your language by scrolling through the menu until your language is selectable.
After the language has been changed accordingly, the remaining content of the screen will now appear in your language.
You now can choose whether you want to **try** Ubuntu or **install** it.
It is advisable to start the **live system** by clicking the button
Try Ubuntu

The advantage of this is that you can get an overview of the system without having to install Ubuntu on the hard disk.
The **live system** is and remains on the stick and does not change anything on your PC.

Nevertheless, you can explore, configure and even install the system.
However, changes in the live system are not permanently saved, so any actions you perform will be lost after reboot.

If you have decided to install Ubuntu 18.04 on your computer, select either

➢ the option to install provided within the live system
➢ after restart > the button **Install Ubuntu**.

*Ubuntu usually gets along well with UEFI. Nevertheless, it is recommended to disable **Secure Boot** in the BIOS.*

7.1. Keyboard layout

Here you can select your **keyboard layout**.

Since the keyboard layouts are different in each country, it is important that you choose a keyboard layout in your language.
The keyboard layout is preset in the language you have selected before.

It is recommended that you use a sample text to check whether the chosen model meets all your requirements.

Type text to test the keyboard.

In this way, you can check whether the individual letters including special characters are displayed correctly.

If you select the wrong keyboard here, you can easily undo this at a later time.

7.2. Installation Selection

7.2.1. Type of installation

The following window offers some basic choices re-
garding the type of installation.

You can choose between

➤ Normal installation
➤ Minimal installation

Minimal installation
No applications are pre-installed.
This gives you a leaner basic system, which you can
expand at a later time according to your individual
needs.

Normal installation
Certain standard applications, such as the Libre-Of-
fice package, are already pre-installed, so you can
start working right away.

The normal installation is convenient because it takes the basic decisions off your hands.
On the other hand, it may install applications that you do not need and thus unnecessarily waste space.
This quick guide describes the **normal installation**.

7.2.2. Other Options

Download updates while installing Ubuntu

Since the ISO file is not always up to date, the installed Ubuntu has to be updated after the first restart.
If you check this box, updates will be downloaded during installation. This saves time.
In my experience, however, a manual update after the first login is necessary even if you check this box.

Install third-party software for graphics and WI-FI hardware and additional media formats

Here you will be asked if you want to install third-party software or not.
Since this type of software may not be pre-installed by Linux distributions for licensing reasons, it is up to you whether you need and want to use proprietary drivers and codecs.
In particular, graphics cards and WLAN cards run better and more smoothly with the third-party software provided.

7.3. Create partitions

7.3.1. Automatic partitioning

So far nothing has been changed on your hard disk.
However, this changes with the next steps.
Partitioning prepares the selected hard disk for the installation of Ubuntu.

Partitioning: the space available on the hard disk is divided into different areas (partitions) and these are adapted in a further step for the actual installation.

I always recommend that beginners provide a separate hard drive for a Linux system.
Although with some experience dual-boot and even multi-boot on a single hard drive is not a problem, there may be some difficulties that may present a novice user with major hurdles.

If there is a hard disk with Windows in your computer, disconnect it temporarily for security reasons so that you don't accidentally delete your Windows system.

Erase disk and install Ubuntu

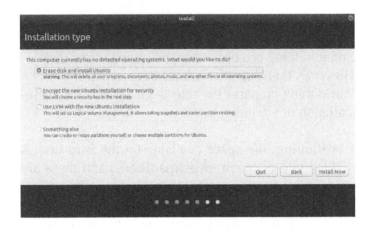

If you have decided to install Ubuntu on a single hard disk next to an existing Windows, the installer automatically detects that an operating system (namely Windows) is already on the hard disk.
In this case, you will be asked if you want to delete Windows or install Ubuntu in parallel.
The next steps are identical.

You can encrypt your system or use the LVM intended for advanced users.

Erase disk and install Ubuntu confirm with **Install now.**
This starts automatic partitioning.In the next window you will be warned that the changes will be written to your hard drive in the next step.

This will delete all the data on it.

So please make sure once again that you have selec-ted the correct hard disk and that there is no data loss when you press **Next**.

If you have selected automatic partitioning, you can jump to chapter 7.4 to continue the installation.

If you want to know how individual partitioning works with ***something else,*** *see* ***chapter 7.3.2***

7.3.2. Individual Partitioning

Individual partitioning makes sense if you want to de-couple your **home directory** (personal folder) from the system.

As already mentioned, when asking about the type of installation, select the **Something different** button.

The first window, which opens in this case, shows you which hard disks are currently installed in your computer and are therefore available for selection.

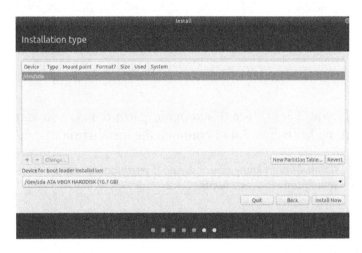

The abbreviation **dev** stands for Device, **sd** means that it is a hard disk.
sda is hard disk **a**.
A second hard disk would be called **sdb**.
If there are several hard disks in the computer, you have to select which of them should be partitioned.
Be very careful because paritioning permanently dele-tes all files.
After you have made the correct selection, create a **partition table**.

To do this, press the corresponding button in the bottom right corner.

New partition table

If there are already partitions on this hard disk, they will be overwritten.

This will be indicated again in the next window.

Confirm with **Next**.

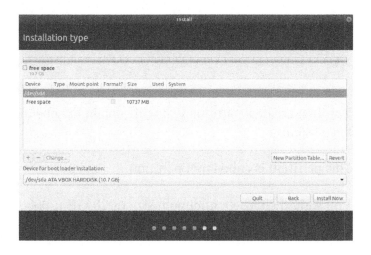

Here you can see how much disk space (MB) is available on the hard disk.

You need a partition for the **operating system**, one for the **home directory** and one for **swap**.

This is nothing else than what automatic partitioning does. The difference is that in this way, you can determine the sizes yourself, while otherwise predefined sizes are used.

7.3.2.1. Root-Partition

Use the **[+] - button** to create the first partition.

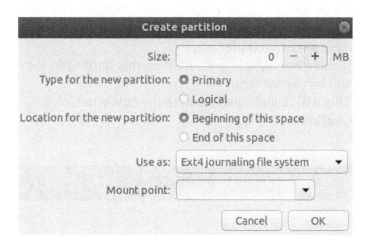

You first create a partition that will contain the operating system.

This partition is called root partition.

You should choose a minimum size of 20 GB (20000 MB) for the root partition.

As **type of the new partition**, select **Primary**.

You need logical partitions if you want to create more than four partitions.

For **use as** select

Ext4 journaling file system.

As **mount point** you choose
/.

Now you will be redirected back to the first window.

The partition for the root directory is now visible in the graphic as a green bar.

The size you have assigned to this partition will also be displayed.

You now can proceed in the same way with the remaining available memory.

Press the **[+]** - button again and repeat the previous steps.

You can now specify the size of the **swap** memory.

7.3.2.2. Swap

For **use as** select
Swap.

Swap is especially important for computers with little RAM (memory).
If the built-in memory in the computer is insufficient for certain actions, the swap area on the hard disk is used as extended memory.
If you notice that this happens more often, you should consider upgrading your computer.

As the size to be set for the swap partition, the rule of thumb was that you should use about twice the amount of the installed memory.
However, this is relativized, the more RAM is actually present in the computer.
This reduces the likelihood that swap will be used at all.
On computers with less than 4 GB of RAM, it is important to set up a correspondingly large swap partition.
Swap becomes less important if you have 16 GB or more in your computer.
If you have selected automatic installation, Ubuntu will create a reasonably large swap file.
If you only define the root and home partitions during manual installation, a swap file will also be created automatically.
4000 MB should be enough swap on newer computers.

7.3.2.3. Home folder

Press the [+] - button again and repeat the previous steps.

Now create the **home directory**.

Your personal data and documents will be stored here.

For **use as** select
Ext4 journaling file system.

Depending on what you plan to do with your computer, the size of this partition should be appropriately generous.
Use the remaining amount of memory.

As **mount point** you choose
/home.

Click on OK to confirm.

After confirming with OK you should see the following window.

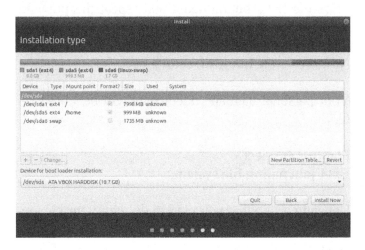

The three partitions are now marked by different colors.

Further information on size and mount points can be
found below in the white box.

You can correct a mistake you find with the **Back**
button.

If not, then confirm with
Install now.

You now can proceed with the installation process.

7.4. Set up the time zone

The hard disk is now partitioned and configured so that Ubuntu can be installed on it.
Before this can happen, however, some information is needed.
In order for the clock to work correctly in the computer, the time zone must be set up.

According to the information provided earlier Ubuntu will recognize where you are.

You can use the map to check if the localization has been correctly detected.

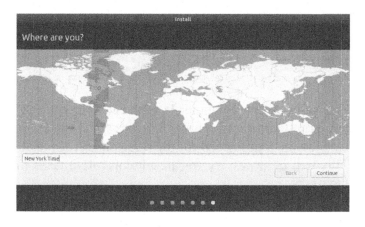

Of course you can change the time zone manually.

7.5. Personalization

In the next step, Ubuntu wants to know

- ➢ your name (your full name),
- ➢ the name of the computer
- ➢ and what your individual username should be

The name of the computer is especially important if you want to become part of a network with your PC.
Now assign a **password** for the selected user name.
This will be necessary for all administrative tasks in the future.
If, in Ubuntu's opinion, the password is too weak for any reason (see above), you will be notified.
A green check mark indicates that everything is alright.
You will need the **password when you log**, if you chose **Require my password to log in**.

If you do not want to log in with a password, simply select **login automatically**.
You can define further users with their own passwords at a later time.

7.6. The actual installation

Now the installation process of Ubuntu 18.04 begins.

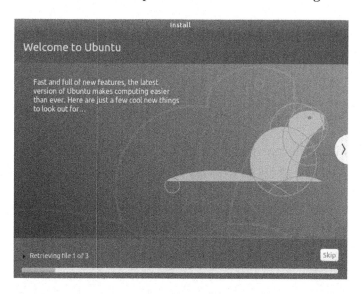

You can use the bar to see how much time is left until the installation is completed.

If you see this window, you have nothing more to do at the moment.

Just wait until the fully automated installation is complete.

7.7. First Start

You will be notified that the installation is complete.

Now you have to **restart** the computer.

Please do not forget to remove the installation stick, otherwise you will end up in the **live system** again.

After restart the login screen will ask you for your the password.

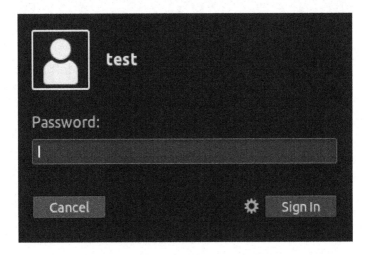

8. Getting started in Ubuntu 18.04

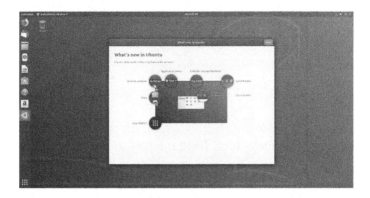

After a short time you are logged in.

The first time you start Ubuntu, you will be guided through some windows, where you will receive basic informations and have to make decisions on certain topics.

8.1. What's new in Ubuntu

In the first window you will be informed about news that show the differences to previous versions of Ubuntu.
This is necessary for Ubuntu 18.04 because it is the first LTS version that has dropped the previous desktop **Unity**.
Ubuntu 18.04. is shipped with the **GNOME**-Desktop.

Press the green **Next**-Button in the upper right corner to proceed.

8.2. Livepatch

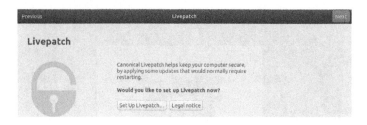

The next window is of little interest to ordinary home users.

You will be asked if you would like to set up a **live patch** for **kernel updates**.

This function is only relevant for computers that should not be switched off over a longer period of time.
You can click **Next** at this point.

8.3. Help improve Ubuntu

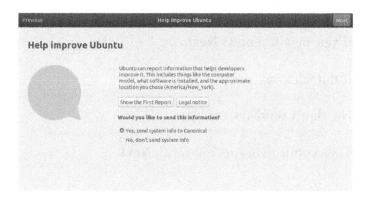

Ubuntu asks you if you agree that certain user data is collected from you.

Most of this information is about your PC (memory, processor, graphics card, etc.).
Personal data is not collected at this point.

Ubuntu justifies this data collection with the fact that valuable information is collected statistically, which ultimately benefits the user.

The default setting is:

Yes, send the system info to Canonical

Please consider carefully whether or not you want to comply with Ubuntu's request for support.

If **yes**, then just press **Next**.

If **not**, choose

No, don't send system info

Then confirm this decision with **Next**.

8.4. Ready to go

The last window will inform you that you are ready to go and that you can immediately install additional applications via the Software Center (Ubuntu software).

If you do not want to install any other applications now, you can close the window with **Done**.

9. Software Updater

After a few minutes, Ubuntu will inform you that updated software is available.
You will be asked if you want to install it.

You update your system with

Software Updater

You can decide if you want to install the suggested updates right away, or if you want to be reminded at a later time.

The update is done automatically by Ubuntu.

As you unfold **details of updates**, you can check details about the updates before starting the process.

10. The GNOME desktop

After completing the initial setup, you can navigate the GNOME desktop and take first steps.
This chapter is for orientation.

10.1. The Dock

On the left side you will see a side bar, that is called

Dock.

The Dock offers you direct access to applications and other important functions of the operating system via buttons.
The dock can of course be configured to your own needs.
Thus, both the appearance and the content of the bar can be changed.
How to do this is described in this chapter.

By default, the sidebar (dock) looks like this:

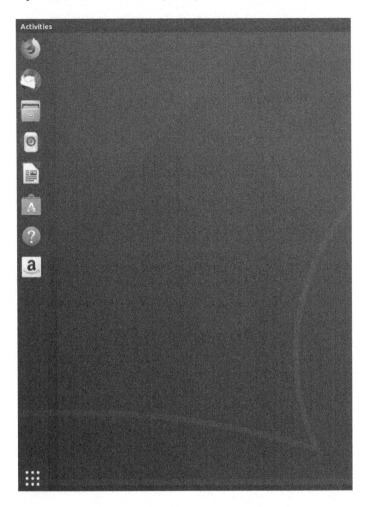

Application launchers are preset for

- ➤ Internet browser *Firefox*
- ➤ Email Client *Thunderbird*
- ➤ File Manager *Nautilus*
- ➤ Word processor *LibreOffice Writer*
- ➤ Music player *Rhythmbox*
- ➤ Software Center *Ubuntu software*
- ➤ Help
- ➤ Amazon Link

Especially the link to Amazon has led to many heated discussions, even if you can remove it easily.

The default buttons are quite useful. Direct access to basic applications is easily possible on this way.

At the very bottom left is the button, which opens the **application overview**

10.1.1. Application Overview

At the bottom left there is a button (grid) which will take you to the **application overview**.

The **application overview** shows all installed applications in alphabetical order.
Just click on the button to start the program.

Unlike other desktop environments, in GNOME applications are not categorized.
For example, **Libre Office Writer** is right next to **Mahjongg**.

In order to find certain programs faster, it therefore makes sense to use the search bar.
This is located in the center at the top of the window.
It is often enough to enter the first letters into the search bar.

GNOME will automatically find any applications that might fit to this input.
For example, typing the letters **f** and **i** in the box will bring up the **Firefox** Internet browser.

If you have installed several applications that start with f and i, you will see all matches. By entering another letter, you narrow down the selection again.

Since there is not enough space to display all installed programs, the content is spread over several pages.
These can be easily selected via the round buttons on the right side.

The filled dot indicates the currently selected page.

In addition, you can either display all applications or only the frequently used ones.
The corresponding buttons can be found below.

10.1.2. Configuration of the Dock

It is very likely that you want to configure the dock according to your own ideas.

You can execute the most important actions directly from the interface.

10.1.3. Remove application launchers

If you have no use for certain applications that are in the Dock, you can of course remove them.
All you need to do is right-click on the corresponding application launcher.
In the pop-up menu the option
Remove from Favorites appears.
This way you remove the button you don't need.

10.1.4. Add application launchers

If you want to add application launchers to the dock, first open the application overview.
All installed applications are displayed here.
A right-click on the applicaton button shows the option in the pop-up menu
Add to favorites

This way, you add the selected application launcher to the dock.

It will initially be displayed at the last position.

10.1.5. Order of the application launchers

To change the order of the application launchers, press the left mouse button and hold it while moving the button to the position you want.

10.2. The Panel

The upper bar (panel) is divided into three areas.

- ➢ Activities
- ➢ Clock, calendar and notifications
- ➢ Status menu

10.2.1. Activities

With the activity button on the far left you can switch to **Overview mode**.

Alternatively, open this window with the **[Super Key]** (also called Windows Key).
This is located between **[Ctrl]** and **[Alt]** and often shows the Microsoft logo.

Type the word **system** into the search bar..

Ubuntu now assumes that you probably want to know something about the system, so it offers you a link to **system monitor**.
Also a link to **system info** will be displayed.

If you type the word **game**, all installed games will be displayed.

10.2.2. Clock and Notifications

If you press the clock in the middle of the top bar, a calendar will open.

In addition to the information on the current date, you will also find a **notification window** here.

10.2.3. Status menu

On the far right is the **status menu**.

Here you can find settings for frequently used functions.

Volume control for the audio system
Network connection and Bluetooth
Information about the registered user
Battery indicator if needed
System features
Button to log out and shut down

10.3. Pre-installed applications

10.3.1. Office applications

Libre Office is a complete office suite with a similar structure to Microsoft Office.
Included are the following single programs:

➢ Libre Office Writer	Word processing
➢ Libre Office Calc	Spreadsheet
➢ Libre Office Impress	Presentation
➢ Libre Office Draw	Drawing
➢ Libre Office Math	Mathematics

The following application is available for viewing PDF documents:

➢ Evince	Documents-Viewer

10.3.2. Multimedia

➢ Rhythmbox	Audioplayer
➢ Totem	Videoplayer
➢ Cheese	Webcam

10.3.3. Graphic applications

➢ Simple Scan	Scanner
➢ GNOME Screenshot	Screenshots
➢ Shotwell	Picture organisation
➢ Eye of GNOME	Picture viewer

10.3.4. System Tools

- ➤ Archive manager
- ➤ Printers
- ➤ Deja Dup   Backup
- ➤ GNOME-Disks
- ➤ Calendar
- ➤ Seahorse   Password Manager
- ➤ Startup Disk Creator
- ➤ Synaptic Package Manager
- ➤ Transmission   BitTorrent-Client
- ➤ Vim   Texteditor
- ➤ gedit   Texteditor
- ➤ Gnome Control Center
- ➤ Software Updater
- ➤ Software and Updates
- ➤ Terminal
- ➤ System Monitor

10.3.5. File Manager

- ➤ Nautilus

10.3.6. Games

- ➤ Solitaire
- ➤ Mahjongg
- ➤ Sudoku
- ➤ Minen

10.4. Workspaces

In Ubuntu 18.04, you can create multiple virtual workspaces.

These are called **workspaces**.

You can open a word processor on one workspace, an Internet browser on a second, and an image editor on a third.

To be able to see the created workspaces, move the mouse cursor to the right edge of the screen in **Activities.**
The **workspace switcher** allows you to conveniently select the desired desktop.

Now open an application on the selected desktop.

You can move content from one workspace to another by holding down the left mouse button.

You can move between workspaces with the following keyboard combination:

[Ctrl] + [Alt] + [Arrow]

11. Software and Updates

You open this very important program via the **appli-cation overview**.

11.1. Ubuntu Software

Here you decide whether you want to use only **open source** (free) software or also **proprietary** software.

Open source means that the source code of a program is openly visible and may be changed.
On the other hand, there are applications where the source code is not open. This applies to all commerci-al programs.
(Microsoft, Apple, Adobe, etc.)

The package sources are preset as follows

> ➤ **main** open source
> ➤ **universal** open source
> ➤ **restricted** not open source
> ➤ **multiverse** not open source

Usually you don't have to change anything here, un-less you only want to use open source software.

Many drivers and codecs, which may be important for the smooth operation of your operating system, will not be available if you decide to use only open soft-ware.

11.2. Updates

Here you determine how updates are to be made.

Automatically check for updates

You can choose between:

➤ daily
➤ every two days
➤ weekly
➤ every two weeks
➤ never

You can specify whether security updates should be downloaded and installed automatically or only displayed.

Most users would like to stay with the selected LTS version of Ubuntu and not switch to one of the intermediate versions.
For this reason, the notifications about new Ubuntu versions are set to only inform you about updates **for long-term support versions**.

The next LTS version will be Ubuntu **20.04**.
So you will not be informed about possible updates to 18.10, 19.04 or 19.10, because these are versions that are only supported for 9 months.
If you still want to switch to such a version, select **For any new version**.

11.3. Additional drivers

Here you can install the proprietary driver for your graphics card if you are not satisfied with the open source driver.

Standard tasks can be done easily with the open source driver, for graphic-intensive applications the proprietary driver is usually better suited.

Ubuntu shows you which drivers are suitable for your card.

All you have to do is select it and then press
Apply changes

12. Software-Center (Ubuntu-Software)

12.1. Installing applications

It is very likely that you need additional software for your individual needs.

For example, there are no applications for graphics editing or video editing.

Unlike Windows, in Linux you don't have to search the Internet for suitable programs. You should even avoid that.
You will find basically everything that is available for Linux in the Ubuntu repositories.

So you get everything from a single source and free of charge in most cases.

By downloading your applications directly from the Ubuntu package sources, they are more trustworthy than much of what you find on the Internet for Windows.

There are several ways to select and install applications.

The easiest way is to use **Ubuntu software**.
Ubuntu software is represented by an orange shopping bag icon in the dock.

Do not be deterred by the shopping bag symbol.
You don't have to buy anything here.

After starting Ubuntu software, you will see an overview that will make it much easier for you to proceed.

The applications in Ubuntu Software are categorized.
This makes the search easier if you don't know what
the programs are called in the Linux world.

You would like to **edit your holiday photos** and are
now looking for an appropriate program.
If you know the name of the application, you can
search for it with the magnifying glass in the upper
right corner.
If you don't know the name, it is advisable to search
for it in the category **Graphics and Photography**.

All programs that are shown to you now have more or
less to do with graphics and photography.
To get more information about a specific application,
simply click on the corresponding button.

Using the example of **Darktable**, I will show you how to easily install the program you have chosen.

Darktable is a powerful photo editing program that lets you edit the brightness, contrast, saturation, exposure and many other settings of your image.

After you have selected **Darktable** in the overview, a window opens which shows you a short description of the application and a screenshot of the program interface.

darktable manages your digital negatives in a database and lets you view them through a lighttable. It also enables you to develop raw images and enhance them in a darkroom.

Other modes besides lighttable and darkroom are a map for geotagging, tethering, print and a slideshow.

darktable supports most modern camera's raw formats, and does all of its processing at very high precision.

In **Details** you will find information about the current version and which source is used for the download.

Opinions and comments can be found in the reviews below.

If you have decided to install this software, all you have to do is click on the button **Install**.

In the following window you will be informed that you have to enter your password. This is the password you set during the installation process and which you also need for log-in.
This prevents software from being installed on your computer without your knowledge and is an important security measure.

You can check the progress of the installation with the help of a bar and the corresponding percentage display.

The installation process usually does not take very long.

You can start **Darktable** immediately from within **Ubuntu-software**.

From now on you can also find the program in the application overview, from where you can select it at any time.

12.2. Remove applications

Ubuntu software allows you not only to install applications, but also to remove them if you don't need them anymore.

To do this, select the **Installed** button in the top center of Ubuntu Software.

The following window will show you all applications that are currently installed on your computer.
Next to it you will see the button labeled **Remove**.

However, please be careful and do not delete applications you do not know exactly which function they have.
In the worst case, deleting important system programs can make the entire operating system unusable.

You can easily delete the Amazon Launcher and the corresponding button. This action has no negative effects on your system.

For information on how to install and remove applications in the **terminal**, please refer to the corresponding chapter.

12.3. Alternative installation options

But Ubuntu software is not the only way to install applications.

Alternatives are:

the program **Synaptic**
> *For experienced users, this program offers a much wider range of functions than Ubuntu software.*
> *However, a certain period of training is required in order to be able to exploit all possibilities.*

the **terminal**
> *The terminal can also be used to install all applications from the Ubuntu package sources.*
> *However, you need to know the exact name of the program.*

13. The File Manager (Nautilus)

The **file manager** gives you easy access to all important places in your system.

In the **file manager** you can

➢ View folders and files
➢ Create folders and files
➢ Move folders and files
➢ Copy folders and files
➢ Delete folders and files

You also have access to the file system.

System configurations are usually done in the terminal or via an editor, but the file manager is usually a good place to get an overview.

The different desktop environments available in Linux usually have their own file managers.
For Ubuntu GNOME, this is **Nautilus**.
The variety of functions is limited compared to other file managers, but should be good enough for most everyday tasks.

Make yourself familiar with this tool, because you will certainly use it very often in the future.

You open Nautilus via the dock by clicking on the **files icon**.

This is what **Nautilus** looks like:

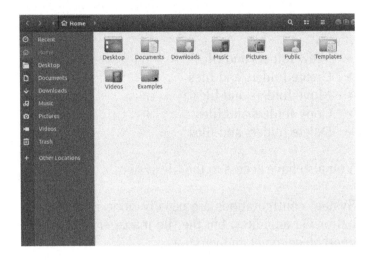

On the left side there is an overview of selectable **directories**.
By default, the home folder is selected here.
To the right you can see the content of the selected directory.

You can see all folders that were created either by the operating system during installation or by yourself at a later time.

13.1. Pre-installed folders

13.1.1. Pictures

Image files are stored in this directory.

13.1.2. Documents

All kinds of documents are stored in this directory. For example, you will find text files or spreadsheets that you create with Libre Office.

13.1.3. Downloads

All files that you download from the Internet can be found in this directory.

13.1.4. Music

Here you will find your music collection.

13.1.5. Public

In this directory you can collect files that you want to make publicly accessible in a network.

13.1.6. Desktop

Any file that you place on your desktop can be found in this folder.
This is because the desktop is only a directory within your personal folder.

13.1.7. Snap

This folder contains all installed Snap applications.

Snaps are a new type of application.
Snaps can be used across platforms, unlike conventional applications, which can be obtained from the Ubuntu package sources.
In addition, snaps give you faster updated versions of applications because they include the necessary dependencies that may be missing on your system.

For many applications, the Software Center (Ubuntu software) provides both an older version from the package sources and a newer snap-version.
You can decide by yourself which version you want to use.
You can also use both at the same time.
However, please keep in mind that a Snap version requires considerably more space on your hard disk than the version from the package-source.

It is possible that the theme you have chosen (appearance) is not supported properly.

13.1.8. Videos

Since there are many useful applications for video editing, it makes sense to create a directory for video files in the personal folder.

Videos that you download from the Internet (please pay attention to copyright) will end up in the downloads folder first, but you can move them to this place at a later time.

13.1.9. Templates

In this folder, you can store all existing or created templates for different applications. This way, you don't have to search for them after you start the program.

13.1.10. Examples

This folder contains contributions for the Ubuntu Free Culture Showcase.

13.2. Configuration of the home folder

Of course, you can design the contents of your personal folder in a completely different way.

13.2.1. Overview

You can:

➤ create additional folders
➤ Create subdirectories
➤ delete existing folders
➤ rename existing folders

Double-click on a directory to display its contents.
These can be individual files or further folders.

The arrows in the upper left corner will help you to navigate.
The right arrow opens the selected directory,
the left arrow leads you back to the starting point.

At the top of the directory list you find the entry
Recent.

Files that you have recently used are stored here.

At the bottom of the directory list you find the entry
Other Locations.

This will take you

- ➤ to the file system (called computer here)
- ➤ to the networks
- ➤ to further hard disks (internal or external)
- ➤ to USB sticks
- ➤ to SD cards

Right-clicking on a directory opens a menu.

- ➤ *Open in the same window (> Open)*
- ➤ *Open in a new tab within the window (> Open in new tab)*
- ➤ *Open in a new window.*

You can **move** or **copy** a directory or a file.

After right-clicking on the directory or the file

➢ Select **Cut** if you want to move the file.
➢ Select **Copy** if you want to copy the file.

The file will be saved in a clipboard.

Now change to the target directory.

With **Paste** (right click on empty area in target folder) you execute the process

You can also move or copy the directory using the commands **Move to** ... and **Copy to** ....

In this case, you must specify a **destination** and confirm the operation with **Select**.

You can **delete** directories and files by moving the selected directory to the trash.

However, this action does not delete it permanently. You can find and restore the file inside the trash at any time.
Only when you click **empty trash** the deletion process will be carried out definitively.

By clicking **Rename** you change the name of a file or directory.

In **Properties** you can view or change the **permissions** of the selected directory.
Here you can specify who else other than you should have full access to the directory.

13.2.2. Creating a new folder

Right-click on the free space in the directory to open another pop-up menu.
Here you can find

New folder

If you click on it, a field with a blank line opens immediately.
Type in the name of the new folder.
By pressing Enter or the **Create** button the folder will be created.

If you change your mind, you can cancel this action at any time. The corresponding button is located on the left side.

You can delete or rename the newly created folder at any time.

13.2.3. Hide the directory list

Press the **[F9]** key to show or hide the directory list. This gives you even more space for the contents.

13.2.4. Enlarge Symbols

With **[Ctrl]** + **[+]** you can enlarge symbols for the folders.
With **[Ctrl]** + **[-]** you reduce the size of the symbols again.

However, only 3 zoom levels are provided.

13.2.5. Create bookmarks

You may want to pin your own directories as shortcuts into the directory list.

To do this, create a new folder named **Test** within the Documents folder.
Then drag this folder into the directory list to **New Bookmarks** by keeping the left mouse button pressed down.

With a right click on this folder (in the directory list) a pop-up menu opens, which offers you to remove the entry again.

13.2.6. Show hidden files

Hidden files are files or folders that are not visible by default.
This is because they are protected against unauthorized or unqualified access in this way.

Your personal settings from various applications are stored as hidden files.

These directories and files are marked with a dot in front of the file name.

The hidden Thunderbird folder with your emails looks like this:

.thunderbird

If you want access to the hidden files for any reason, use a keyboard shortcut.

[Ctrl] + [H] makes all invisible files and directories visible.

14. Settings

14.1. General Settings

The Ubuntu Gnome desktop doesn't offer as many possibilities to customize your system as some other desktop environments.

However, there are several interesting configuration options available in **Settings**.

To open **Settings**, start the **application overview** and press the button

Settings.

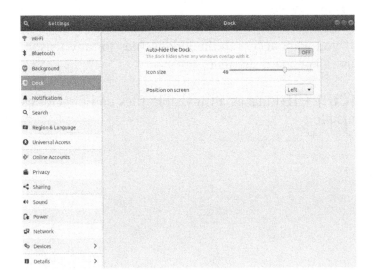

WI-FI and Bluetooth

Set up and configure your WI-FI and bluetooth here.

14.1.1. Changing the desktop background

The **Background** button allows you to change your **desktop background** and the **lock screen** wallpaper.

If you click on the default image, a selection of diffe-rent background **Wallpapers** appears immediately, from which you can choose one.

If you select **Pictures** you can include your own pho-tos.
In this case you should make sure that your picture fits to the resolution of your monitor.

If you do not like images as desktop background, it is also possible to select only a **solid color**.

14.1.2. Lock screen

The **lock screen** is activated after a pre-defined period of inactivity to save energy.

Of course, you can change the default settings.

Simply click on the button
Power,
which you will find further down on the left.

The selection menu next to
Blank screen
allows you to specify when the blank screen is to be
activated.
You can deactivate this function by choosing
Never

For the Background of the **lock screen**, you can either use the same wallpaper as for the desktop or define a different one.

➢   *Ubuntu wallpapers*
➢   *Pictures (Own photos)*
➢   *colors*

14.1.3. Configuring the Dock

Dock Configuration

14.1.4. Auto-hide the Dock

Here you will find a switch that is set to Off by default.

The dock will always remain visible, even if you open the window to fullscreen.

If you set this function to ON, the Dock will be hidden whenever windows overlap with it.

This means that a maximized window will fill the entire screen.
If you close the window again, the Dock will reappear.

14.1.5. Icon Size

The default setting is 48 pixels.

You can adjust the size of the icons in the dock with a slider.
The fewer pixels you choose, the smaller the icons will be.
The change does not only affect the icons themselves.
The width of the dock is also adjusted automatically.

14.1.6. Position on Screen

You may not like the fact that the Dock is located on the left side of your screen and is displayed vertically.

You can change this setting here.
The Dock can also be placed at the bottom or at the right.

14.1.7. Notifications

By default, your system provides you with up-to-date information of all kinds.
One of the most important of these notifications is the information that system updates are available.

However, you can also deactivate these notifications completely.

In the corresponding menu, you can see two buttons at the top.
The upper one refers to notifications in the running system, the second to notifications that appear on the lock screen.

You can also configure the notification settings in detail for various applications.
To do this, simply click on the ON button for one of the applications listed below.
A new window will open listing various options.

For example, you can switch on and off **sound alerts** for notifications.

If you only want to be informed about system updates, just switch all other applications to OFF and the Software Updater to ON.

14.1.8. Search

Ubuntu 18.04 has a powerful search bar.

In Settings you can specify in which categories you want Ubuntu to search when you start a query.

➢ Files
➢ Calendar
➢ Passwords and Keys
➢ Terminal
➢ Ubuntu software

14.1.9. Region & Language

The language settings have been configured according to your specifications during the installation process.

The operating system should be set in your language and the keyboard configuration should be designed for your chosen model.

If you would like to change these settings, you can do that in this menu.

14.1.10. Universal Access

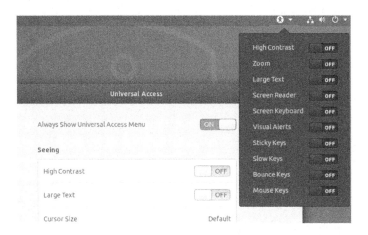

Ubuntu has put a lot of work into universal access features.
By default, these features are disabled.

You can display the accessibility menu in the upper bar by switching **Always show universal access menu** to ON

A small icon (little man) appears in the bar, which opens a menu with the most important configuration settings.

The settings in the configuration menu are summarized under different categories.

➢ Seeing
➢ Hearing
➢ Typing
➢ Pointing and Clicking

You can set a higher contrast or change the size of the mouse cursor.
You can use an on-screen keyboard and **AccessX** provides a comprehensive typing assistant.

14.1.11. Online Accounts

Connecting to different **online accounts** is no problem in Ubuntu.

To do this, enter your access data and connect to the selected online service.

Various services such as Nextcloud or Facebook are available.

14.1.12. Privacy

Screen lock

You can automatically lock the screen while you are not present. This is controlled by the corresponding switch button. In addition, you can also determine the time at which the screen is switched off when you are not present.

Location services

These services allow applications to recognize your geographic location. However, you must explicitly allow this feature. The corresponding switch is set to OFF by default to protect privacy!

Usage and History

Here you can specify whether the history should be saved and for how long. The default setting is ON.

Purge Trash & Temporary Filess

With this function you can empty the trash automatically and also delete the temporary files. You can set a time period for this to happen. The selection in the pop-up menu ranges from 1 hour to 30 days.

Problem Reporting

If you want to send error reports to Canonical, activate this item.
You can also specify whether this should be done automatically, or if you want to be asked beforehand.

Connectivity Checking

This function is intended to detect possible network problems.

14.1.13. Sharing

This feature allows remote users to view and control your screen.

This can be useful if you have your computer serviced.
By default, however, the switch is set to OFF.

14.1.14. Sound

This is the center for your sound configuration.

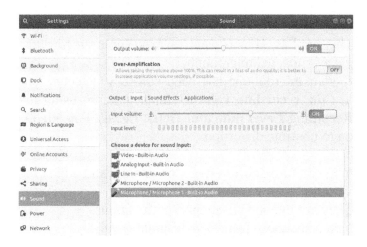

At the top you will find the fader for the **output volume** of your audio applications.
This can be a Youtube video in your browser or the mp3 file on your hard drive.

You can adjust the volume to over 100% using the **Over-Amplification** button. However, this can lead to distortions. Therefore it is better to leave the button OFF.

In **Output** you define the output assignment. This can be an internal sound generator, but also an external device that you have connected via a socket.
Ubuntu usually recognizes which options are available to you.

In **Input** you define the input channel for audio recording.
This applies, if you want to make voice recordings via a connected microphone.
If your microphone has been correctly detected, adjust the **recording volume** (Input volume) using the Recording **Level indicator** (Input Level). Pay attention to possible distortion.

You can turn **sound effects** on and off and adjust the volume.
They are intended to support notifications.
You can choose from five different sounds.

14.1.15. Network

Set up your network here.
The wired connection is automatically detected by Ubuntu during installation.
WI-FI is recognized correctly in most cases, but you will need your password to get access to it.

You can also set up VPN (Virtual Private Network) or a network proxy.

14.2. Devices

In **Devices** you will find everything that has to do with your external hardware.

14.2.1. Displays

Ubuntu usually detects the **resolution** of your monitor automatically.
But you can change it at any time.

Scaling allows you to enlarge the displayed screen content. You can choose between 100% (default) and 200%.

Night Light displays the screen in warmer colours. This is to protect the eyes.

Manual: You can set an individual time, when this should happen and for how long.

From sunset to sunrise:
Night mode is automatically controlled by the time zone you select.

14.2.2. Keyboard

In this menu you will find the predefined keyboard shortcuts.

Scroll down a bit in the selection list.

Maximize window:

[Super] + [Arrow up]

This means that you must press these two buttons **simultaneously** to maximize the currently open and active window.

[Super] The Windows Button
[Arrow up] Arrow key up

If you want to reset the window back to its original size, press

[Super] + [Arrow down]

You can set up individual keyboard shortcuts.
To do this, just double-click on the desired action. You will then be prompted to press the desired key combination.
Confirm with **Define**.

14.2.3. Mouse & Touchpad

Here you can change some basic settings that affect your mouse.

14.2.4. Primary Button

Left-handers can swap the right and the left mouse button here.

14.2.5. Mouse

Here you can adjust the mouse speed with a slider to your needs.

Natural Scrolling:
This reverses the scroll direction when scrolling with the middle wheel of the mouse.
The default direction is reversed if you set the button to ON.

14.2.6. Printers

Normally the printer is recognized automatically and you don't have to set anything up yourself.
If you want to add a printer, press the corresponding button and make sure that the printer is connected and switched on.

Ubuntu will guide you through the necessary steps.

14.2.7. Removeable Media

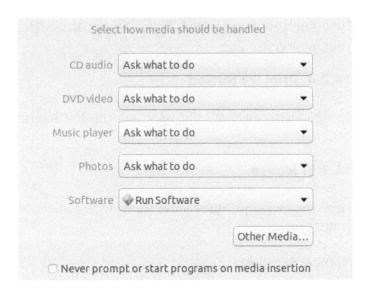

This menu allows you to define what should happen when you insert removable media.

The default setting is **Ask what to do**.

However, you probably want, for example, an inserted audio CD to be started and played always with the same program.

You can select your preferred application here.

Ubuntu will make suggestions as to which installed program might be suitable for the selected media.

However, you can select **another application**.

In addition to the media listed here, you will find more options under **Other media**.

You can also specify the corresponding programs for Blue Ray media or e-book readers.

Leave **devices** by pressing the arrow in the upper left corner.

Now you are in **Settings** again.

At the bottom left you will find **Details**.

14.3. Details

14.3.1. About

In **About** you will find general information about

➢ the device name you have chosen
➢ the installed memory
➢ the processor of your computer
➢ graphics
➢ the GNOME version
➢ the type of operating system
➢ the disk on which Ubuntu is installed.

You can also check for updates here.
After pressing the Check for Updates button, the Software Center will open and show you available updates.

14.3.2. Date & Time

Normally, the system automatically determines the date and time according to the time zone you selected.

The **time zone** was set during installation.

The button for the automatic determination of the time zone is set to OFF, because this would require the determination of your current location via the Internet.
To protect your privacy, you should always leave this button in this position.

You can change the default settings manually at any time.
This may be necessary if, for example, you are in a different time zone but do not have access to the Internet.

You also can change the **time forma**t from 24-hour cycle to 12 hours (AM/PM).

14.3.3. Users

Here you can change all personal information

Change the user name
All you have to do is enter the new name in the line provided.

Change the password
To do this, you must first enter the previous password. Enter the new password in the next line. Ubuntu will give you instructions on how to create a password that is as secure as possible. Click Change to confirm your decision. You can cancel the action at any time by clicking Cancel.

Upload a picture
Ubuntu offers a selection of images, but you can also upload your own.
This image can be displayed on the login screen each time you log in.

Enable automatic login
The button is set as you selected it during installation.

14.3.4. Default Applications

Here you specify which installed applications should be used for certain tasks by default.

If you install several web browsers, you can specify which one will be started when you open a link from outside (e.g. link in e-mail).

The same applies to the other default applications.

These defaults are especially important if you have installed several different applications that all have the same or a similar function.

Clicking on a photo will automatically open the program you set here.
This can be a image viewer or an image editing program like GIMP.
Depending on whether you want to view pictures only or edit them immediately, you make the appropriate selection here.

15. Gnome Tweaks

An extension that is available in the Software Center allows you to configure your system much more than with **Settings**.

Open Ubuntu software and type **tweaks** in the search bar.
This application is also called GNOME Tweak Tool and allows you to customize advanced GNOME settings.

The next step is to install this program.
When the installation process is finished, you will find it in the application menu.

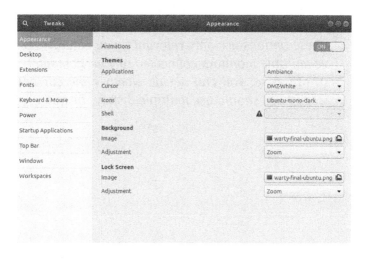

Tweaks is structured similarly to **Settings**.
On the left side you will find different categories, on the right side in the main window the corresponding configuration options.

15.1. Tweak the workspaces

Dynamic Workspaces

Workspaces can be created and removed as required.

Static workspaces

The number of available workspaces is determined beforehand.

Number of workspaces

If you have chosen static workspaces, you can specify how many you want.
This selection is not available if you have chosen dynamic workspaces.

Display handling

These options are only relevant if you actually have multiple monitors connected to your computer.
In this case, you can decide whether the current workspace should use multiple dispays or not.

15.2. Desktop

Here you can specify which **icons** should be displayed on your desktop.

The first button determines whether you want to display icons in general or not.

If this button is set to OFF, the other options are not available.

If this switch is set to ON, you can decide individually whether to display the following four destop icons.

Home

Since the home folder icon is usually already in the dock, it is not very useful on the desktop.

Network Servers

This icon is only relevant if you have set up a network and want to access it from your desktop.

Trash

A trash can on the desktop may be useful.

Mounted Volumes

These can be external hard disks, USB sticks, CD-ROMs or SD cards.
If you want immediate access to these data carriers, you should set the Button to ON.

15.3. Appearance

Here you can change the **appearance** of the whole distribution.

Be sure to remember what the default settings were like so you can always return to the original state if you don't like the new settings.

You can change the overall look of your system with **themes**.

You can select all themes installed on your system. Some are already pre-installed, but you can install many additional themes via Synaptic or the terminal.

Changing the theme affects the whole system.

If you choose a dark theme (Adwaita Dark), then all backgrounds and window borders will be dark.

This affects the file manager, the configuration menus and all applications.

Ambiance :

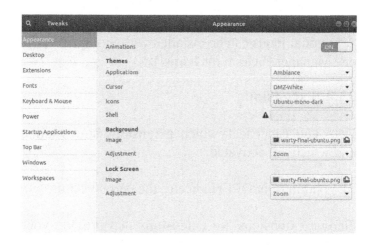

Adwaita Dark :

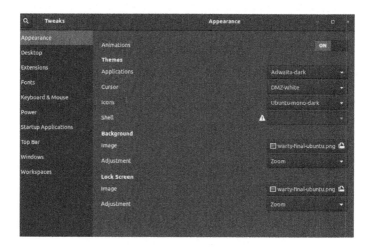

As you can see, not only the color of the background changes.
Even the buttons to close and minimize the window are completely different.

In addition, you can also select another mouse cursor and change the icon set.

Additional Icons can be installed with **Synaptic** Package Manager (Search for **Icons**!).

15.4. Extensions

Here you can check which **extensions** are installed and which are activated.

The button (ON/OFF) indicates the current status.

Gnome extensions are **extensions** that provide your system with additional functions.
You can decide for yourself whether you need the offered functions or not.

However, you will not find the extensions in the system by default. They are not an official part of Ubuntu.

All available Extensions can be found on the GNO-ME website.

https://extensions.gnome.org

Please keep in mind, however, that this is third-party software.
A proper integration into the system is usually given, but a certain risk remains.
There are several ways to download this software.

15.4.1. Method 1

You can download the extensions directly from the website.

However, some additional steps are necessary.

First, you need to integrate the **GNOME Shell Integration** add-on into your browser.

For Firefox, click on the button with the three dashes at the top right.
In the menu you will find the item **Add-ons**.

In **extensions** you can search for the add-on and install it.

You also have to make preparations in the system it-self.

In the terminal, use the command

```
sudo apt install chrome-gnome-shell
```

to install an additional small program that allows you to download directly from the website.

15.4.2. Method 2

You select the desired extension on the website and then search for it in the Software Center.

On this way you do not need the steps that are necessary to install directly from the browser.

Please keep in mind that none of these extensions are included in the official Ubuntu package sources.
Therefore, Ubuntu does not guarantee that they will work properly.

15.4.3. Example for an extension

Frippery applications menu

This extension replaces the activity button (top left) with an application menu.

After installing
Frippery applications menu
you need to restart the computer.

The activity button has disappeared.

Instead, you'll find an **application menu** that classifies your installed programs into categories, making them easier to find.

However, the functions that are covered by Activities disappear.

15.5. Windows

Here you can configure the behavior of the windows to your needs.

15.5.1. Window Focus

The configuration of window focus determines,

➢ whether a window is to be activated by clicking with the mouse (click to focus)
➢ whether a window should be activated by moving the mouse pointer over it (Sloppy)
➢ whether a window is to be activated by moving the mouse pointer over it and loses focus again when the pointer moves over the desk. (secondary-click)

15.5.2. Titlebar Actions

Titlebar Actions determines what should happen if you double-click, middle-click or secondary-click (right mouse button) with your mouse on the bar.

Double-Click can cause,

➢ that the window is maximized to screen size (toggle maximize)
➢ that the window is minimized and therefore disappears. (minimize)

15.5.3. Titlebar Buttons

If you don't like the fact that the buttons of the title bar for closing, minimizing and maximizing are on the right side, you can move them to the left side by placing them with the selection button (Left/Right).

In addition, you can delete both the Maximize and Minimize buttons completely from the bar by simply dragging the corresponding Button to OFF.

15.6. Top Bar

Here you can activate or deactivate some additional functions for the top bar.

This is controlled by ON/OFF-Buttons.

You can hide the application menu, which shows the currently open applications in the upper bar.

If you are using your computer with a battery, you can display the remaining percentage of the battery charge.

In addition to the time in the middle of the bar, you can also display the date.

You can add the week numbers to your calendar.

15.7. Fonts

If you don't like the fonts used and the size you can change the font settings here.

The **window title** preset for the fonts:

> ➤   ***Ubuntu***   *Name of the Font*
> ➤   ***11***   *Font size*

Remember the default settings and try out different options in this menu until you like the selection you have made.

Confirm changes with the green **Select** button.

You should not change **Hinting** and **Antialiasing**, as optimal values are usually set here.

The **scaling factor** is a powerful tool.

The default setting is **1**.

You can scale up or scale down the screen content by changing this value.

15.8. Startup Applications

Specify here which applications should start automatically each time the operating system is started.

By pressing the **plus button (+)** you can select the desired application.

If you select **Firefox,** the browser will start automatically after each login.

The selection can be undone by pressing the **Remove** button.

15.9. Keyboard & Mouse

Here you you can configure additional features for the behaviour of Keyboard & Mouse.

16. Windows Applications in Linux

There is no direct way to install **Windows applications** on a Linux operating system.

Programs such as Microsoft Office or Adobe Photoshop are not provided for Linux.

However, there are ways you can still use these applications on Linux.

There are two different ways you can try out.

16.1. Wine and PlayOnLinux

The application **Wine** creates a Windows runtime environment on your Linux computer.
It tries to simulate a Windows environment as realistic as possible.
This works well for some applications, less for others.

The best way to install the Wine-Frontend **PlayOnLinux** is via the Software Center.
You can also load and install **Wine** itself, but PlayOnLinux simplifies the handling of Wine with an intuitive and graphically appealing menu navigation.

After the first start, an attractive user menu awaits you, which gives an initial overview of the possibilities of PlayOnLinux.

The applications recommended by POL are divided into categories.

For example,in **Office** you will find several versions of Microsoft Office.

However, the latest version 2016 is missing.

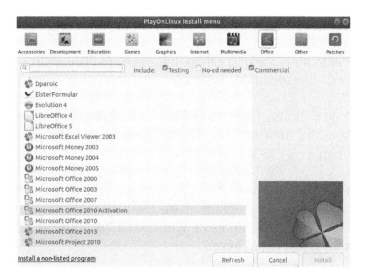

Please keep in mind that you will need an original DVD/CD and the activation key to install an application.

Once you have decided on a program, start the installation with the **Install** button, which you will find at the bottom right.

During the installation, you may be notified that additional files are required to complete the installation successfully.

In this case, follow the instructions.

It is advisable to visit the Wine website.

https://www.winehq.org/

In **AppDB** you can check whether the application you want to install is well supported by Wine or not.
There is also a ranking based on the experience of users.
Platinum is the best rating, but there are also applications that are rated as garbage.

You will also find tips and hints on what you have to consider for a successful installation of a desired program.

PlayOnLinux lists many well-known and frequently used Windows programs in the categories.
However, you can also try to **install an application that is not listed here**.

To do this, click on the left bottom corner on **Install a program that is not listed**.

This can work in some cases, but usually you have to do some research how to install the application and all dependencies correctly.

Unfortunately there are some applications which cannot be installed this way or which are only of limited use despite successful installation.

If you are not successful with Wine, you could try the commercial program **Crossover**.
However, Crossover is not available free of charge and there is no guarantee that it will work better.

16.2. Virtual Maschines (Virtual Box)

Another way to make Windows programs or MacOS applications run is to set up a **virtual machine**.
In a virtual machine not only a runtime environment is set up, as is the case with Wine.
You install a real Windows or MacOS within your Linux operating system, which is completely independent.
You need an original CD/DVD and the activation key.

You have to provide this operating system, which runs parallel to Ubuntu, with enough cpu and memory, otherwise the virtual machine is only usable to a very limited extent.
For a virtual machine with Windows, you should provide at least 50 GB of your hard disk space.
Therefore, increase the value suggested during installation accordingly.

There are several ways to create a virtual machine on your system.
One of the most common is Virtual Box.
You can find this program in the Ubuntu repositories.
Via the **Ubuntu Software** you can install **Virtual Box** conveniently on your computer.

Virtual Box is also available for Windows and MacOS.
You can also go the other way around and install Ubuntu in
the Virtual Box under Windows.

After starting Virtual Box, click the NEW button.

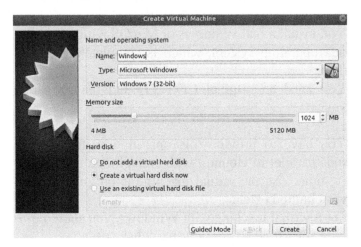

Give the operating system an individual name and
increase the memory within the green area.
The value selected here will no longer be available to
your main system when you start the virtual machine.

In the next window, you specify where this virtual
machine should be stored.
You can also specify the file size (the amount of
space on the hard disk).
You will then be guided through the installation process without any problems.
It makes sense to install the **Virtual Box Extensions**
in addition, as this considerably extends the range of
functions.

17. The Terminal

The terminal is the interface that connects the user directly with the operating system.

There is a specific command for each action you want to perform.

This command can be executed by entering it in the command line and confirming with ENTER.

To open the terminal, go to the application overview and type the first three letters (ter).
The **terminal** is now listed as an application.

After starting the terminal, you will only see one line.
It shows your user name, followed by the name of your computer.
The username in this example is **test**.
The user **test** is logged in to the (@)**test-computer**.

The following character ~ stands for the place inside the computer where we are at the moment.

~ is the abbreviation for the personal folder.

You now can enter the required command where the cursor is located.

Some important examples:

Updating the repositories
```
sudo apt update
```

Updating the system
```
sudo apt upgrade
```

Installing a program
```
sudo apt install [Program name]
```

After entering these commands you will be asked for the password.
This is necessary for security reasons to prevent unauthorized access to your system.

The list of available commands is endless

You can copy, move and delete files.
You can also use the terminal as a file manager, since you can query the contents of directories with simple commands.

In many cases, the terminal is even the more effective and faster way to perform certain tasks.
However it is very important that you know the commands and that you are able to use the keyboard quickly.

18. Ubuntu Derivatives

There are also other official versions of Ubuntu. They use a different desktop than GNOME.

You can choose between

Kubuntu
Ubuntu with KDE Plasma

Ubuntu Mate
Ubuntu with Mate Desktop

Ubuntu Budgie
Ubuntu with Budgie Desktop

Xubuntu
Ubuntu with XFCE Desktop

Lubuntu
Ubuntu with LXDE desktop

Ubuntu Studio
Ubuntu for multimedia applications

In addition, there are numerous independent distributions based on Ubuntu.

Elementary OS, Linux Mint, KDE Neon and Peppermint are just a few examples.

19. Outlook

Meanwhile there is already Ubuntu 18.10.
This version is more current, but is only supported for 9 months.

Ubuntu 19.04 will be released in April 2019.
This version has a support of only 9 months.

Version 19.10 with short-term support is out since October 2019.

The next LTS version is 20.04. It will be supported for 5 years.
Wih the release of Ubuntu 20.04 you can decide whether you want to use 18.04 until the end of support in 2023 or upgrade to the newer LTS version.

It is possible at any time to switch to the short-term versions and upgrade to the next after expiration.
In this case, however, you leave the LTS path.

Also available:

Arch Linux - Quick Guide for Beginners

Bibliographic information of the German National Library:
The German National Library lists this publication in the German National Bibliography;
Detailed bibliographical data can be found on the Internet at http://dnb.dnb.de .

Notes

Notes

Made in the USA
Monee, IL
21 October 2020